This bite-sized book []
useful overview of w;
help you achieve the

- Learn how to use
  can be more prou
- Identify time wasters and explore ways to
  reduce them
- Recognise the reasons why you may
  procrastinate
- Clarify and prioritise your objectives and goals
- Be more assertive and establish boundaries
- Know how to work smarter rather than harder

CW00695132

Time is more valuable than money.
You can get more money,
but you cannot get more time

Jim Rohn

Time is precious

Imagine if time was a bank account and each morning you were credited with 86,400 seconds. If, by the end of that day, you hadn't spent any of the credits then they would instantly be deducted from your account. What would you do?

It is highly likely that you would make every effort to take care of those seconds and invest them wisely. It is interesting though how much time can be taken for granted and those seconds become lost or wasted.

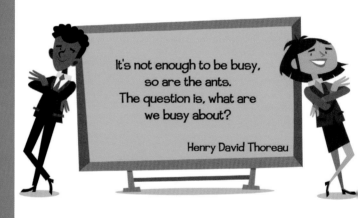

It's not enough to be busy,
so are the ants.
The question is, what are
we busy about?

Henry David Thoreau

Living in the busy ages

Time pressure seems to be the norm for so many people in the modern world. Internet connection speeds and computing power are increasing exponentially, along with an endless amount of information and entertainment. It can often feel as if there is so much to do and so little time.

You may well feel that life in the "busy ages" is a constant bombardment of information and overwhelming choice, which can lead to feelings of overstimulation and agitation. Taking time out to stop and reflect on what is making you busy is a great place to start.

It's how we spend our time
here and now, that really matters.
If you are fed up with the way
you have come to interact
with time, change it

Marcia Wieder

Time management and stress

Time pressure is one of the biggest precursors to unhealthy stress levels. It can prompt feelings of personal inadequacy and impact on your self-esteem and confidence. This can lead you towards stress burnout which is a state of emotional, physical and mental exhaustion caused by excessive and prolonged stress.

Great time management is essential if you want to handle a heavy life load, without experiencing unhealthy stress. Learning how to manage your time will give you more confidence and direction, when you have too much going on. It will also help you to feel calmer, more in control and ultimately less stressed.

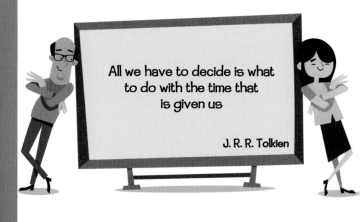

All we have to decide is what
to do with the time that
is given us

J. R. R. Tolkien

The benefits of time management

Great time management will give you more control of your time and energy. It will help you to focus on activities, people and projects that make the biggest impact in your life.

Getting on top of your time management will also assist you in achieving your goals in less time and with less effort, whilst creating a better life balance. The following pages offer some simple tips and suggestions for improving your time management skills.

How to manage your time well

Declutter

Creating an environment around you that provides more space, energy and clarity will impact on your health, happiness and overall well-being. It will help you to be more organised and productive.

The tidier and the more minimalistic you are, the easier it will be to find things and this can save lots of time. It is also good to declutter your mind, as this will help you to focus better and feel more in control. Decluttering, on a regular basis, can be very therapeutic and provide you with an energising sense of achievement.

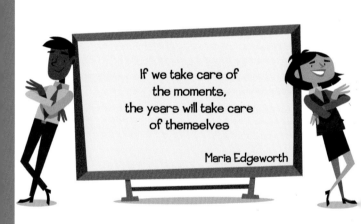

If we take care of
the moments,
the years will take care
of themselves

Maria Edgeworth

Conduct a time audit

We are creatures of habit and a great deal of what we do, we do on autopilot. The first step to improving your time management is to find out where your time actually goes. You may think, for example, that you only spend 30 minutes on a task, when in reality it is taking a lot longer.

One way to keep track of your time is to download one of the many excellent apps that help you to track everything you do, for a week. You will then be able to access a report to find out what is consuming your time. With this information, you can start to make the necessary adjustments and improvements.

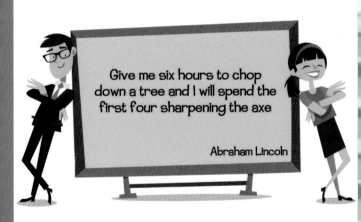

Give me six hours to chop down a tree and I will spend the first four sharpening the axe

Abraham Lincoln

Plan your day

Aimlessly wandering into your day may be a lovely thing to do when on holiday or even on your day off; however, to get things done, planning your day is essential. Creating to-do lists for each goal and project, by listing all the measurable steps that need to be achieved, is an excellent place to start and this will save you time in the long run.

Taking time to plan your day will also help keep you focused and motivated, as you will then be able to monitor what you have already achieved. It will help you to feel more in control and on top of things.

Take a rest; a field that has
rested gives a bountiful crop

Ovid

Schedule in rest time

Creating moments of sanctuary in your day, and scheduling in proper breaks, is a great way to reenergise and refocus. Going immediately from one meeting or task to another can be exhausting. It is far more constructive to take some time to have rest stops, so you can clear your mind and relax.

Doing focused breathing exercises, meditation or even a bit of desk yoga has been scientifically proven to be very effective for managing stress levels. A great way to clear your head and replenish your energy is to go outside and get a blast of fresh air.

Get into good habits

With so many people now spending more time working from home, it can be easy to get into bad habits. Bringing your work into the bedroom will blur the boundaries and make you feel sluggish.

To feel fresh and alert, start your day the way you want it to continue and get up and get going. Doing a fake commute to work by getting washed and dressed and then walking around the block will help you to get in the right frame of mind for the working day ahead.

Set yourself SMART goals

It is important to bear in mind that you can't manage something you don't measure and you won't be able to improve on something that you don't properly manage. A great way to plan what you are setting out to achieve is to set SMART (Specific, Measurable, Achievable, Relevant and Timed) goals.

Setting SMART goals involves working through each of those five components to build a measurable goal that embraces what needs to be achieved. This approach will eliminate guesswork and generalities and help set a clear timeline. It will also make it easier for you to track progress and identify missed milestones.

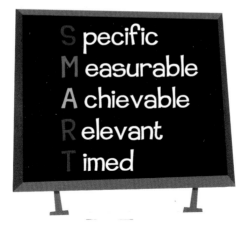

Procrastination is the
thief of time

Chinese Proverb

Eat the frog

Mark Twain once said that if the first thing you do each morning is to eat a live frog, you can go through the day with the satisfaction of knowing that is probably the worst thing that is going to happen to you all day long.

Your "frog" is your biggest, most important task, the one you are most likely to procrastinate on. It is very tempting to put off what you don't like doing to another time, or even another day or week. If you tackle it first thing, it won't be hanging over you and you will feel so much lighter and more motivated as a result.

Done is better than perfect

Sheryl Sandberg

Avoiding chasing perfectionism

A desire to do your best is an admirable quality and, of course, there are some situations where cutting corners is not an option. It is important, however, to work out whether there are occasions when you waste time, and resources, attempting to achieve perfectionism in absolutely everything you do.

Reversioning something time and time again, or getting bogged down in analysis paralysis, can be both stressful for you and others around you. There will be instances where a particular task is simply better done than perfect.

Boundaries are a part of self-care.
They are healthy, normal,
and necessary

Doreen Virtue

Establish boundaries

Establishing and maintaining personal time boundaries is key to a healthy, fulfilling and productive life. If you feel obliged to say yes to all demands that are put upon you, then you will become a receptacle for other people's agendas.

It is important to take ownership for your choices and make sure that when you say yes to others, you are not saying no to yourself. Having respect for your own time encourages others to do the same.

Meet to get things done

It is important to remember that successful and time-savvy people schedule or attend meetings to get things done, not to just make an appearance. When you are involved in any meeting, be very clear about the value you can add.

Establishing the overall goal of the meeting is a good place to start and setting an agenda pre meeting helps everyone to prepare and stick to the agenda. Gathering materials in advance is useful too and may even save time on having to be involved in any follow-up meetings.

Expect the unexpected

It is inevitable that you will be faced with unexpected requests and surprises during the day. It is important, on that basis, to build in some contingency time. Being flexible and willing to adapt will help you to feel less stressed if this happens.

You also need to be careful to not be reactive; decide when these things need to be done and add them to your list. If something is urgent and important, then review your priorities and do it straight away, if possible. If it can wait, then stay focused on what you were doing.

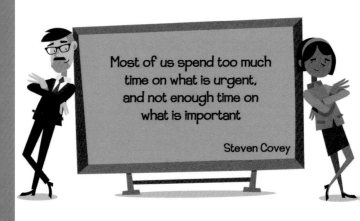

Most of us spend too much time on what is urgent, and not enough time on what is important

Steven Covey

Understand how to prioritise

Identifying the difference between what is important and what is urgent will help you to be less reactive and more responsive. It will also enable you to overcome the natural tendency to focus on unimportant urgent activities.

Important activities have an outcome that will lead you towards achieving your goals. Urgent activities demand immediate attention, and are often associated with achieving someone else's goals. A useful tool that can help you with this is known as "The Eisenhower Matrix" and is well worth looking into.

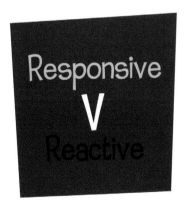

Delegate

Sometimes you may find you are overwhelmed with tasks and simply have too many balls in the air. This may be a good time to look at what you can delegate and give someone else the responsibility for a particular function, task or even decision.

Delegation can be challenging because it means you will have to trust someone else to do something for you and that may not come easily. Delegating, however, will give you the time and ability to focus on higher-level tasks. It will also help you to develop trust and improve communication with other people in your life.

Be decisive

One big time bandit can be indecision. A logical and systematic decision-making process will help you to address the key elements that result in making a decision. Here is a useful 6-step critical-thinking path that can help:

1. Identify your decision and establish your objective
2. List the various options that you have available
3. Gather as much information as you need on all of them
4. Conduct a risk analysis and weigh up the pros and cons of each
5. Select the best option and develop a plan of action
6. Implement your decision and stick with it, with a willingness to learn as you go

33

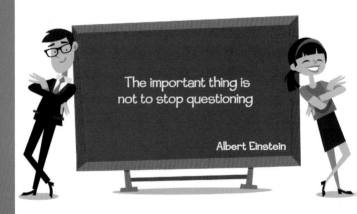

The important thing is
not to stop questioning

Albert Einstein

Question your performance

Building in reflection time, to review and challenge what you do, is the key to eliminating bad habits and improving your time management. By revisiting your to-do lists at the end of the week, you can ask yourself these questions:

- Which tasks took longer than I expected?
- Why did they take longer than I thought?
- Was I unrealistic in my expectations when I set the original goal?
- What support can I get to make improvements?
- How am I managing my stress and energy levels?
- What have I achieved that I am proud of?

Nothing is a waste of time if you use the experience wisely

Rodin

Celebrate time well spent

Sometimes it can be easy to just move on to the next task, without relishing what you have achieved. There is a good reason why it is important to take time out to savour success and it is to do with the chemicals in your brain.

When you anticipate achieving something, or you take time to recognise those achievements, dopamine, one of the quartet of chemicals responsible for your happiness, is released. This is something that will make you feel good, so take the opportunity to celebrate success, whenever you can.

Yesterday is gone.
Tomorrow has not yet come.
We have only today.
Let us begin

Mother Teresa